Farm Animals

Written By:

Kim Mitzo Thompson

Karen Mitzo Hilderbrand

Illustrated By:
Mark Paskiet

Cover Design:
Steve Ruttner

Visit Our Web Site at
http://www.twinsisters.com

Twin 418 - **Farm Animals (Tape/Book Set)** - ISBN# 1-882331-86-9

Twin Sisters Productions - 1340 Home Avenue Suite D Akron, OH 44310 (800) 248-TWIN

Table of Contents

Six Little Ducks

Six little ducks that I once knew,
Fat ones, skinny ones, fair ones too,
But the one little duck with the feather on his back,
He led the others with a quack, quack, quack!
Quack, quack, quack, quack, quack, quack!
He led the others with a quack, quack, quack,!

Down to the river they would go,
Wibble wobble, wibble wobble, to and fro,
But the one little duck with the feather on his back,
He led the others with a quack, quack, quack!
Quack, quack, quack, quack, quack, quack!
He led the others with a quack, quack, quack,!

Home from the river they would come,
Wibble wobble, wibble wobble, ho-hum-hum!
But the one little duck with the feather on his back,
He led the others with a quack, quack, quack!
Quack, quack, quack, quack, quack, quack!
He led the others with a quack, quack, quack,!

Old MacDonald's Letter Farm

Old MacDonald had a farm,
A B C D E.
Letters, letters in the hay,
F G H I J.
With a...
K L M N O P,
Pigs and ducks and bumblebees.
Q R S T U & V,
W X Y Z!

A B C D E F G,
Letters I can sing.
H I J K L M N,
Soon I'll learn to read.
With a...
O P Q, R S T, U V W, X Y Z.
Learn your letter names with me.
The animals like to read.

Cows and horses in their stalls,
Sing their letter names.
Chickens cluck the alphabet,
Learning is their game!
From A B C to X Y Z,
Learn them and you will succeed.
Old MacDonald guarantees
Learning is the key!

Old MacDonald had a farm,
A B C D E.
Letters, letters in the hay,
F G H I J.
With a...
K L M N O P,
Pigs and ducks and bumblebees.
Q R S T U & V,
W X Y Z!

Bought Me A Cat

1. I bought me a cat and the cat pleased me,
   I fed my cat under yonder tree.
   Cat goes fiddle-i-fee.

2. I bought me a hen and the hen pleased me,
   I fed my hen under yonder tree.
   Hen goes chimmy-chuck, chimmy-chuck,
   Cat goes fiddle-i-fee.

3. I bought me a duck and the duck pleased me,
   I fed my duck under yonder tree.
   Duck goes quack, quack,
   Hen goes chimmy-chuck, chimmy-chuck,
   Cat goes fiddle-i-fee.

4 ...goose goes hissy, hissy...
5 ...sheep goes baa, baa...
6 ...pig goes oink, oink...
7 ...cow goes moo, moo...
8 ...horse goes neigh, neigh...
9 ...dog goes bow-wow, bow-wow...

 Twin 418 - Farm Animals

Have You Ever, Ever, Ever?

Have you ever, ever, ever, ever, seen a purple pig,
Wearing pink pajamas while doing a jig?
No I've never, ever, ever ever seen a purple pig,
Wearing pink pajamas while doing a jig.

Have you ever, ever, ever, ever, seen a dancing cow,
Wearing cowboy boots and courtin' a sow?
No, I've never, ever, ever, ever, seen a dancing cow,
Wearing cowboy boots and courtin' a sow.

Have you ever, ever, ever, ever, seen a singing duck,
Wearing high heel shoes while driving a truck?
No, I've never, ever, ever, ever, seen a singing duck,
Wearing high heel shoes while driving a truck.

Have you ever, ever, ever, seen a horse that was green,
And liked to read lots of magazines?
No, I've never, ever, ever, seen a horse that was green,
And liked to read lots of magazines.

If you've never, ever, ever, ever, seen a purple pig,
And you've never, ever, ever, ever, seen a dancing cow,
And you've never, ever, ever, ever, seen a singing duck,
And you've never, never, ever, seen a horse that was green,
Then just what have you seen?

Well I've never, ever, ever, ever, seen a purple pig,
And I've never, ever, ever, ever, seen a dancing cow,
And I've never, ever, ever, ever, seen a singing duck,
And I've never, ever, ever, seen a horse that was green,
But what I've seen you won't believe.

Have you ever, ever, ever, ever, smelled the summer breeze,
Or looked at the sun and started to sneeze?
Have you ever, ever, ever, ever, seen a butterfly,
That was soaring way up in to the sky?
Have you ever, ever, ever, ever, seen a rainbow,
Just after the rain had stopped to flow?
Have you ever, ever, ever, ever, watched the ocean tide
Appear before your very eyes?

All these things that I've shared with you are just as special as the things
you've viewed. If you look around at the world you'll see...

beauty guaranteed!

6   Twin 418 - Farm Animals

The Farmer In The Dell

The farmer in the dell,
The farmer in the dell,
Heigh -ho, the derry-o,
The farmer in the dell.

The farmer milks the cow,
The farmer milks the cow,
Heigh -ho, the derry-o,
The farmer milks the cow.

3. The farmer feeds the pigs, etc.
4. The farmer shears the sheep, etc.
5. The farmer plants the seed, etc.
6. The farmer plows the field, etc.
7. The farmer cleans the barn, etc.
8. The farmer combs the horse, etc.

Make up your own verse!

Can You Name That Animal Sound?

Let's take a trip to Mr. Conway's farm and learn all about the animals.
Let's play with the chicks and chase the pigs and learn the animal sounds.
The pigs are oinking. The cats are meowing.
The horses are neighing, and the chickens, they like to cluck.

Each animal makes such a special noise, that is how they talk.
Each animal learns to communicate, with grunts and chirps and squawks.
The birds are chirping. The dogs are barking.
The cows are mooing, and the chickens, they like to cluck.

Now Mr. Conway, feeds those animals and cleans and scrubs their pens.
He plays with the dogs, combs the horses, and collects eggs from the hens.
The sheep are baa-ing. The ducks are quacking.
The mosquitoes are buzzing, and the chickens, they like to cluck.

The farm is filled with animal sounds, Mr. Conway would agree.
Can you name the animal sounds? It's an animal symphony.
Can you name this sound?... Right! The pigs go ...
As they roll in their muddy pens.

Can you name this sound?... Right! The ducks go ...
As they waddle under the fence.

Can you name this sound?... Right! The horses go ...
As they gallop around the farm.

Can you name this sound?... Right! The dogs go ...
As they chase and tease the cats.

Can you name this sound?... Right! The sheep go ...
As the farmer sheers their wool.

Can you name this sound?... Right! The chickens go ...
As they sit upon their eggs.

Can you name this sound?... Right! The cats go ...
As they chase the little mice.

Can you name this sound?... Right! The cows go ...
As they feed their calves fresh milk.

Can you name this sound?... Right! The birds go ...
As they fly around the farm.

Can you name this sound?...Right! The mosquitoes go...
As they buzz around your ear.

It's time to leave Mr. Conway's farm we've learned a lot today.
Each animal makes a special sound, from a moo to a cluck to a neigh.
Each animal makes a special sound, from a moo to a cluck to a neigh.

Grandpa's Farm

I went to the farm and asked my old grandpa to show me a thing or two.
I went to the farm and asked my old grandpa to show me a thing or two.
I thought we would ride a horse, play in the barn, or drink pink lemonade.
But Grandpa's ideas were not part of mine. The work he started to find!

I went to the farm and asked my old grandpa to show me a thing or two.
I went to the farm and asked my old grandpa to show me a thing or two.
The field needs a plowin', your grandma's a hollerin', the animals all need fed.
So follow my lead and help your old grandpa. We're planting the field with seed.

I went to the farm and asked my old grandpa to show me a thing or two.
I went to the farm and asked my old grandpa to show me a thing or two.
A bucket of seed was placed in my hand, a shovel, and gloves for the job.
I looked at my grandpa. He started to grin, for the work was about to begin.

I went to the farm and asked my old grandpa to show me a thing or two.
I went to the farm and asked my old grandpa to show me a thing or two.
I planted the seed and stopped for a rest. The job was just about done.
My grandpa he nodded and waved to me. Now the animals we must feed.

I went to the farm and asked my old grandpa to show me a thing or two.
I went to the farm and asked my old grandpa to show me a thing or two.
The pigs were a squealin', the feed I was wheeling into their messy pens.
Then Grandpa did look and said with a smile, "Come rest with your grandpa awhile."

I went to the farm and asked my old grandpa to show me a thing or two.
I went to the farm and asked my old grandpa to show me a thing or two.
We drank lemonade under the shade while we felt the warm summer breeze.
My grandpa and I just started to sigh for the work was finally through.

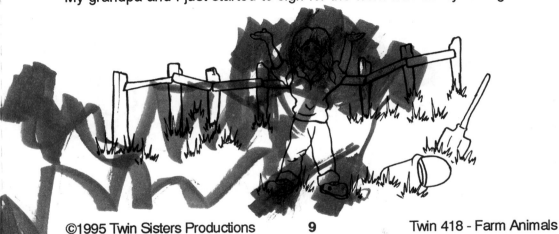

Farmer Grumble

There was an old man who lived in a wood as you can plainly see,
Who said he could do more work in a day than his wife could do in three.
"If that be so," the old woman said, "Why this you must allow,
That you shall do my work for a day while I go drive the plow."

"But you must milk Tiny the cow for fear she should go dry,
And you must feed those little pigs that are within the sty,
And you must watch those speckled hen or she will run away,
And you must wind that reel of yarn that I spun yesterday."

The woman took her staff in her hand and went to drive the plow,
The old man took the pail in his hand and went to milk the cow.
But Tiny hinched and Tiny flinched and Tiny wrinkled her nose,
And Tiny gave the man such a kick that blood ran down to his toes.

'Twas, "Hey, my good cow," and "Ho, my good cow,"
And "Now, my good cow, stand still.
If ever I milk this cow again, it be against my will."
Then he went to feed the pigs that stand in yonder sty,
He bumped his head against the post and how the blood did fly.

And then he watched the speckled hen for fear she'd run away,
But he forgot that reel of yarn that his wife had spun yesterday.
He swore by all the leaves on the tree and all the stars in heaven,
That his wife could do more work in a day than he could do in seven.

But The Farmer Just Went To Bed

The farmer went to milk his little cow,
The farmer went to milk his little cow,
The farmer went to milk his little cow,
But the cow had run away.
The farmer chased the cow around,
The farmer chased the cow around,
The farmer chased the cow around,
But the cow he got away.

The farmer went to ride his little horse,
The farmer went to ride his little horse,
The farmer went to ride his little horse,
But the horse had run away.
The farmer chased the horse around,
The farmer chased the horse around,
The farmer chased the horse around,
But the horse she got away.

The farmer went to feed his hungry pigs,
The farmer went to feed his hungry pigs,
The farmer went to feed his hungry pigs,
But the pigs had run away.
The farmer chased the pigs around,
The farmer chased the pigs around,
The farmer chased the pigs around,
But the pigs they got away.

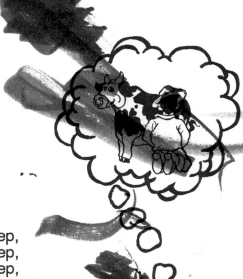

The farmer went to shear his woolly sheep,
The farmer went to shear his woolly sheep,
The farmer went to shear his woolly sheep,
But the sheep had run away.
The farmer chased the sheep around,
The farmer chased the sheep around,
The farmer chased the sheep around,
But the sheep they got away.

The farmer saw his wife appear just then,
The farmer saw his wife appear just then,
The farmer saw his wife appear just then,
And she turned around and said...
"The cows need milkin' and the pigs need fed,
Did you ride the horse or shear the sheep instead?
There's so much work; quit scratching your head!"

But the farmer just went to bed!

Had A Little Rooster

1. Had a little rooster by the barnyard gate,
   That little rooster was my playmate,
   That little rooster went cock-a-doo-dle doo,
   dee doo-dle-dee, doodle-dee-doo-dle dee do.

2. Had a little cat by the barnyard gate,
   That little cat was my playmate,
   That little cat went meow, meow, meow,
   That little rooster went cock-a-doo-dle doo,
   dee doo-dle-dee, doodle-dee-doo-dle dee do.

3. Had a little dog by the barnyard gate,
   That little dog was my playmate,
   That little dog went arf, arf, arf,
   That little cat went meow, meow, meow,
   That little rooster went cock-a-doo-dle doo,
   dee doo-dle-dee, doodle-dee-doo-dle dee do.

4....duck went quack, quack, quack...
5....pig went oink, oink, oink...
6....sheep went baa, baa, baa...
7....cow went moo, moo, moo...
8.... horse went neigh, neigh, neigh...

Help The Farmer Find The Cows

Draw a line through the maze to the cows.

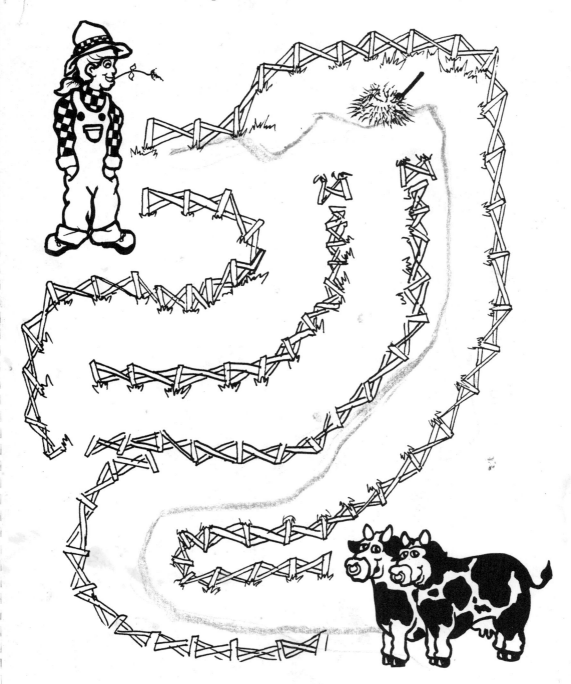

Connect The Dots From A-Z.

Connect the dots from A-Z. Color.

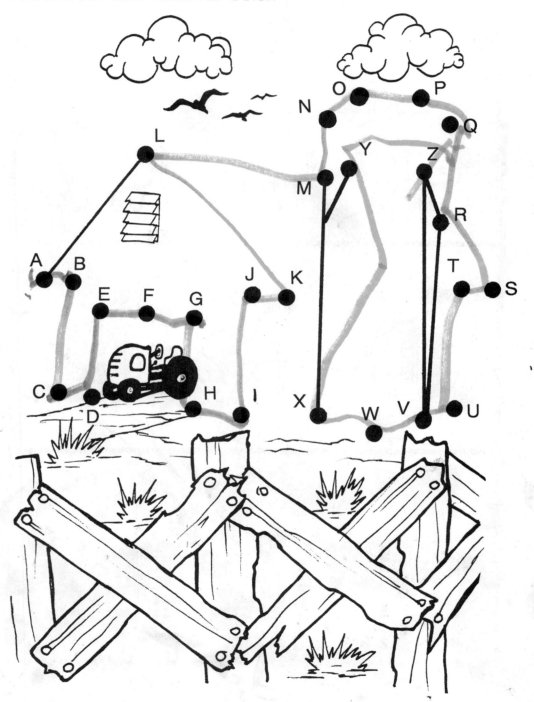

Find The Lambs That Are Alike

Circle the two lambs that are alike in each row.

Adding Is Fun

Draw a line from each problem to the correct answer.

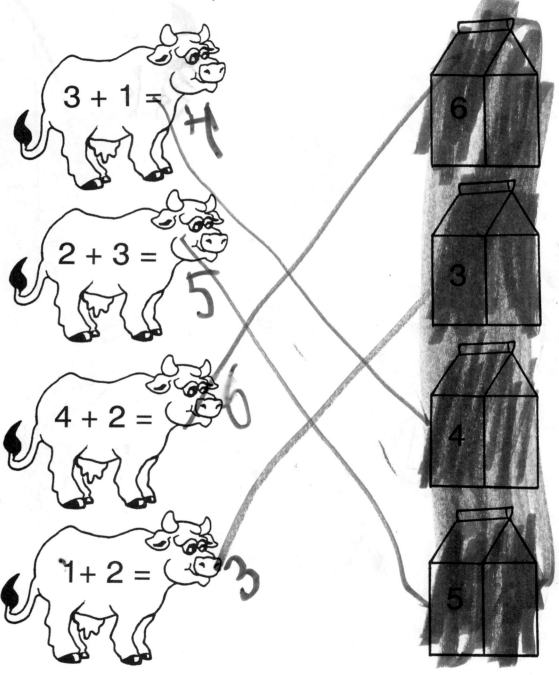

Matching Letters

Match the upper case letter to the correct lower case letter.

Animal Puzzle

Can you find these words?

Help The Pigs Find The Corn

Draw a line through the maze to the corn.

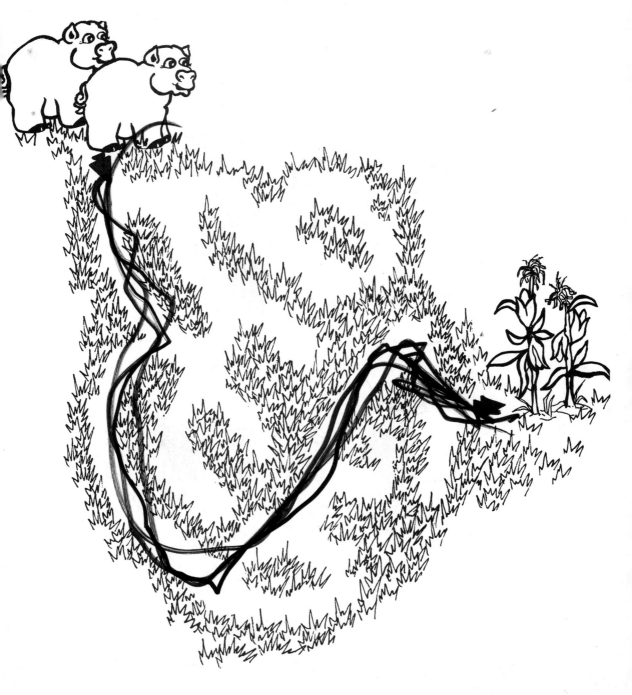

Help The Mother Chicken Find Her Chicks

Draw a line through the maze to the chicks.

Baa, Baa, White Sheep

Reproduce the sheep pattern. Cut out the pattern.
Have the children put cotton on the sheep's body to make
their own white sheep.

Connect The Dots From 1-20

Connect the dots from 1-20. Color.

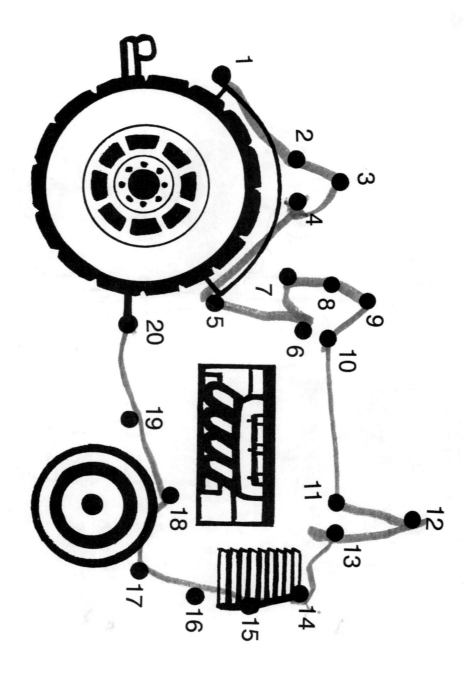

Help The Chicken Find Eight Eggs.

Help the chicken find 8 eggs. Color.

The Sound of "H"

Circle the pictures that begin with the sound of "h" like horse. Color.